EDUCATIONAL COSTS, PRICES AND FINANCIAL AID

EDUCATIONAL COSTS, PRICES AND FINANCIAL AID

REBECCA R. SKINNER
AND
BLAKE ALAN NAUGHTON

Nova Science Publishers, Inc.
New York

For permission to use material from this book please contact us:
Telephone 631-231-7269; Fax 631-231-8175
Web Site: http://www.novapublishers.com

LIBRARY OF CONGRESS CATALOGING-IN-PUBLICATION DATA

Educational costs, prices, and financial aid / Rebecca R. Skinner and Blake Alan Naughton (editors).

p. cm.

ISBN 978-1-60456-644-4 (softcover)

1. College costs--United States. 2. Student aid--United States. I. Skinner, Rebecca. II. Naughton, Blake Alan.

LB2342.E398 2008

378.3'8--dc22 2008018771

Published by Nova Science Publishers, Inc. ✢ New York

CONTENTS

PREFACE*

The rising cost of attending U.S. colleges and universities is a growing concern, as most Americans believe that college is out of financial reach for qualified students. For federal policymakers, concerns focus on issues of affordability, access for low-income students, and whether federal student financial aid is keeping pace with rising prices. This report presents the current status and historical trends of college costs, with an emphasis on the prices undergraduate students are ultimately charged at the varying types of institutions of higher education and how they pay for postsecondary education using student financial aid.

College tuition and fees have been rising more rapidly than household income over the past two decades. In 2005-2006, the average price charged for tuition, fees, room, and board at four-year public and private institutions was $17,447 — a 577% increase from 30 years ago. On the basis of the mean household income of a household in the bottom fifth of the population, the price of college in 2005 was 71.3% of their income.

Historically, congressional involvement with issues of college costs and prices has focused on issues related to student access to postsecondary education. However, as Congress has considered the reauthorization of the Higher Education Act (HEA), attention has been given to additional actions that could be taken at the federal level to address college costs and prices. Actions considered have included creating price indices, providing incentives for controlling costs, making it easier for students to earn college credits, reducing regulatory burden, and increasing the availability of relevant public information. It is not clear which of these strategies would be most effective at addressing the issue of college costs or prices, or whether some of these strategies would be more effective if implemented at the state or institutional level. As Congress continues to debate the reauthorization of the HEA, an expanded federal role regarding college costs and prices may be considered.

* Excerpted from CRS Report RL34224, dated October 30, 2007.

This report begins by exploring three core concepts: college cost (what institutions spend), sticker price (what students are charged), and net price (what students actually pay) — defining each and presenting current and historical data. This information is followed by a discussion of various influences on costs and prices. The report concludes with an overview of relevant issues for reauthorization of the Higher Education Act of 1965 (HEA, P.L. 89-329 as amended by P.L. 105-244). Where data are available, this report considers all types of postsecondary education institutions: public, private not-for-profit, and private for-profit institutions.

Chapter 1

INTRODUCTION

The rising cost of attending U.S. colleges and universities is a growing concern, as three out of five Americans believe many qualified people will not have the opportunity to pursue a college education, and a large majority of Americans believe that the students who do make it to college have to borrow too much to go.[1] For students and their families, these concerns raise questions as to whether they will be able to afford a college education and whether their choice of postsecondary institutions is limited by price. For federal policymakers, concerns focus on issues of affordability, access for low-income students, and whether federal student financial aid is keeping pace with rising prices.

The public, lawmakers, researchers, and the higher education community offer numerous theories as to why the costs of providing a college education continue to rise, but there is little consensus as to either root causes or ways of mitigating the problem. This report presents the current status and historical trends of college costs, with an emphasis on the prices students are ultimately charged at the varying types of institutions of higher education (IHEs) and how they pay for postsecondary education using student financial aid. Although prices are certainly an issue for graduate and professional education, the focus of this report is on undergraduates, particularly full-time undergraduates.[2]

College tuition and fees have been rising more rapidly than household income over the past three decades. In the 1976-1977 school year, the average price charged to students for tuition, fees, room, and board at four-year public and private institutions was $2,577; in 2005-2006, it was $17,447 — a 577% increase.[3] Looking at family resources to pay for college, from the mid-1980s to the mid-1990s, tuition and fee levels averaged across public and private four-year institutions and public 2-year institutions increased by 41%.[4] During the following decade, they increased by 36%. Mean household income, on the other hand, increased by 9% and 10% respectively. The divergence is particularly pronounced for low-income households. For households in the bottom fifth of the population, their mean household income increased 5% from the mid-1980s to the mid-1990s and declined by 0.4% during the following decade.

In general, a complex set of factors affects college prices directly and indirectly, making it hard to say definitively what are the underlying causes of price increases. This complexity, coupled with the tremendous diversity of institutions that constitute postsecondary schools, makes it difficult to determine what can or should be done about the issue of rising college prices.

Historically, congressional involvement with issues of college costs and prices has focused on issues related to student access to postsecondary education. However, as Congress has considered the reauthorization of the HEA, attention has been given to additional actions that could be taken at the federal level to address college costs and prices. Actions considered have included creating price indices, providing incentives for controlling costs, making it easier for students to earn college credits, reducing regulatory burden, and increasing the availability of relevant public information. It is not clear which of these strategies would be most effective at addressing the issue of college costs or prices or whether some of these strategies would be more effective if implemented at the state or institutional level. As Congress continues to debate the reauthorization of the HEA, an expanded federal role regarding college costs and prices may be considered.

This report begins by exploring three core concepts: college cost (what institutions spend), sticker price (what students are charged), and net price (what students actually pay) — defining each and presenting current and historical data. This exploration is followed by a discussion of various influences on costs and prices. The report concludes with an overview of relevant issues for reauthorization of the Higher Education Act of 1965 (HEA, P.L. 89-329 as amended by P.L. 105-244). Where data are available, this report considers all types of postsecondary education institutions: public, private not-for-profit, and private for-profit.

DEFINITIONS OF COST AND PRICE

In discussing how much it costs to attend college, how much it costs to educate students, or how much families need to save for college, it is critical to distinguish between two concepts: cost and price. College *costs* generally refer to what institutions spend to provide education and educational-related services to students. *Price* commonly refers to what students and their families are charged for higher education and what they pay. As discussed throughout this report, these amounts are not necessarily the same.

Three distinctions are frequently made in the definition of price. First, there is *sticker price*. This is the tuition and fees that institutions charge (e.g., the published price). The second distinction is the *total price of attendance*, which is often referred to as the *cost of attendance* (COA).[5] This includes the tuition and fees that institutions charge students as well as other expenses related to attending that institution. These expenses may include room and board for on-campus housing, rent for off-campus housing, books, and transportation. A third distinction in the definition of price involves *net price*. This is what students pay after financial aid is deducted from the total price of attendance.

Educators and policy makers commonly look at the effects of net price in two ways. The first is a measure of *affordability*, subtracting only *grants* from the total price of attendance. Loans remain in the total price of attendance for this measure, as loans must ultimately be repaid by the student or student's parents. This may affect decisions to attend college if students and their families are considering the overall out-of-pocket (today or future) price of college attendance. The second is a measure of *access*, subtracting *all* financial aid, including loans, from the total price of attendance. This measure focuses on the amount of money a student would need to attend college in a given year, without considering how much money will ultimately have to be repaid over time. Students generally are awarded financial aid based on merit or financial need. These awards may take various forms, including grants, loans, and subsidized work opportunities. Thus, financial aid may increase access to postsecondary education but not necessarily reduce the ultimate price students will pay to attend.

For the purposes of this report, the term price generally refers to the sticker price. References are also made to net price, but the specific net price measure considered depends on the data that were available for the analysis.[6]

Chapter 2

COST OF A COLLEGE EDUCATION

Few students in American higher education are asked to pay the full cost of their education. Although tuition and fees are an important source of revenue at all types of institutions, other sources of revenue help defray the total costs, and students are then asked to pay significantly less. As shown in table 1, for public institutions, the primary source of subsidy revenue is state appropriations (and local appropriations for some community colleges), and public institutions are increasingly relying on private philanthropic support and endowment income as well. Private non-profit institutions rely heavily on donations, income earned from endowments, supplements from affiliated religious organizations, and other sources of support. Private for-profit institutions, by contrast, are most likely to be tuition dependent and to have few other sources of revenue. Two approaches to cost — revenues and expenditures —are discussed below, because both are used in discussions of college costs; however, references to college costs in the remainder of this report refer to expenditures.[7]

REVENUES

Sources of revenues for institutions of higher education have shifted over time and vary by type of institution. Table 1 shows revenue sources by institution type for 2003-2004, the most recent year for which data are available. The greatest revenue source for public institutions was from state support, amounting to 28% of revenues.

Without large public appropriations, private institutions are more tuition-dependent than public colleges. Sixteen percent of public institutions' revenues come from tuition and fees, but approximately 29% of private not-for-profits' revenues and 90% of for-profits' revenues are from student tuition. In addition, not-for-profit institutions realize 35% of their revenues from private donations and endowment income.

The mix of revenue sources has also changed over time. For public institutions of higher education, direct state appropriations (not including state-funded grants and contracts) have risen from $19.0 billion in 1980-1981 to $53.9 billion in 2003-2004 — but this represents a decrease in *share* of revenues, from 44% to 24%.[8] Although state support has grown over the past 25 years, public college budgets have grown faster and have come to depend more heavily on sources other than appropriations. Private support, from donations and endowment income, has grown from 3% of public college revenues in 1980-1981 to 7% in 2003-2004.[9] Even as colleges aggressively seek increased private support, over the past two decades, tuition has accounted for an increasing share of revenue. At public institutions, tuition and fees comprised 13% of revenues in 1980-1981, compared to 16% in 2003-2004.[10]

Expenditures

Economist Howard Bowen developed the "revenue theory of costs." The theory states that college revenues determine college expenditures. That is, institutions attempt to raise as much money as possible and then spend the money on various activities including teaching, research, administration, and service. According to this theory, a single standard could not be used to determine how much college *should* cost, as colleges make expenditure decisions on the basis of their particular circumstances.[11]

Postsecondary institutions' expenditures generally are grouped into several broad categories: educational and general (E and G) expenditures, auxiliary enterprises, independent operations, hospitals, and other expenditures. The E and G expenditures category includes the majority of institutional expenditures across all types of institutions and is part of total current-fund expenditures (table 2). The E and G expenditure category includes several subcategories such as instruction, research, public service, academic support, student services, institutional support, operation and maintenance of plant, and scholarships and fellowships.

In 2003-2004, total expenditures for degree-granting institutions were about $315.5 billion, and educational and general expenditures were about $239.2 billion, or about 76% of total expenditures (table 2). Considering a fall 2003 enrollment of 16.9 million students,[12] this represents overall expenditures of $18,670 per student and E and G expenditures of $14,150 per student.

Table 1. Total Revenues of Degree-Granting Institutions, by Source of Funds and Type of Institution, 2003-2004

Source of Revenue	Public		Private Not-For-Profit		Private For-Profit	
Total Revenue	$221,921,288	100%	$134,230,762	100%	$8,989,815	100%
Student Tuition and Fees	35,150,615	16%	38,505,631	29%	8,049,205	90%
Public Support	114,167,293	51%	20,277,057	15%	456,940	5%
Federal Appropriations, Grants, and Contracts	*33,053,729*	*15%*	*18,335,784*	*14%*	*397,828*	*4%*
State Appropriations, Grants, and Contracts	*61,417,171*	*28%*	*1,455,556*	*1%*	*59,112*	*1%*
Local Appropriations, Grants, and Contracts	*14,888,344*	*7%*	*485,717*	*0%*	—	*0%*
Capital Appropriations	*4,808,048*	*2%*	—	*0%*	—	*0%*
Private Gifts, Grants, and Contracts	8,335,856	4%	15,847,571	12%	7,079	0%
Investment Income	7,164,011	3%	30,896,917	23%	16,813	0%
Auxiliary Enterprises and Educational Activities	17,907,947	8%	13,616,026	10%	377,860	4%
Hospital Sales and Services	19,587,282	9%	9,657,753	7%	—	0%
Other	19,608,284	9%	5,429,805	4%	81,918	1%

Source: ED, Digest 2006, Tables 337, 341, and 343.

Notes: Student Tuition and Fees is net of allowances and discounting. Federal support does not include student financial aid. Private Gifts includes permanent endowment gifts and capital gifts. State support for private for-profit institutions includes local support. Capital appropriations is from all sources.

Table 2. Total Expenditures of Degree-Granting Institutions, by Type of Expense and Type of Institution, 2003-2004

Type of Expense	All Institutions		Public		Private Not-For-Profit		Private For-Profit	
Total Expenditures	$315,449,161	100%	$205,068,500	100%	$104,317,870	100%	$6,112,791	100%
Education and General	239,159,124	76	154,407,339	75	79,277,972	76	5,473,813	90
Instruction	*92,425,380*	*29*	*56,767,947*	*28*	*33,909,179*	*33*	*1,748,254*	*29*
Research and Public Service	*44,420,273*	*14*	*30,390,403*	*15*	*14,011,883*	*13*	*17,987*	*0*
Student Services, Academic, and Institutional Support	*93,003,018*	*29*	*59,076,305*	*29*	*30,255,172*	*29*	*3,671,541*	*60*
Net Grant Aid to Students	*9,310,451*	*3*	*8,172,682*	*4*	*1,101,738*	*1*	*36,031*	*1*
Auxiliary Enterprises	26,455,268	8	15,705,951	8	10,508,719	10	240,598	4
Hospitals	26,846,098	9	18,471,970	9	8,374,128	8	—	0
Independent Operations	4,959,779	2	736,799	0	4,222,980	4	—	0
Other	18,078,891	6	15,746,441	8	1,934,070	2	398,380	7

Source: ED, Digest 2006, Tables 347, 353, and 354.

Notes: For public institutions, Institutional Support includes physical plant and other operating expenses. Net Grant Aid to Students includes scholarships and fellowships, but excludes allowances. For public institutions, Other includes interest, non-operating expenses, deductions, and depreciation.

Spending on instruction was fairly similar across institutions, accounting for about one-third of expenditures at public (28%) and private not-for-profit institutions (33%).[13] At public and private not-for-profit institutions, spending on instruction accounted for the largest or nearly the largest proportion of expenditures. While instruction also accounted for 29% of expenditures at private for-profit degree-granting institutions, expenditures for student services, academic support, and institutional support composed the largest proportion of expenditures (60%).[14]

One aspect of institutional expenditures particularly relevant for net price (after deducting grant aid) are institutional expenditures for student support (table 2). Scholarships and fellowships[15] accounted for 3% of expenditures at public degree-granting institutions in 1980-1981, increasing to 4% by 2003-2004.[16] At both private not-for-profit and for-profit institutions, net grant aid (excluding allowances) accounted for 1% of expenditures in 2003-2004.

Chapter 3

STICKER PRICE OF A COLLEGE EDUCATION

The price of higher education has increasingly become a topic of both public and congressional debate. It should be noted, however, that during the 2007-2008 academic year, over half of full-time undergraduates at all four-year institutions attended institutions charging less than $9,000 in tuition and fees.[17] At four-year public institutions, 45% of full-time undergraduates attended institutions charging less than $6,000. While $6,000 or $9,000 may still be more than most students can afford to pay, the issue of price may be more productively viewed through this lens rather than one colored by the relatively high prices of the most selective institutions in the country. Only 9% of undergraduates attended institutions charging more than $30,000 for tuition (all of which are private institutions).

There are also public misconceptions about the price of college. For example, a study conducted for the American Council on Education found that the general public substantially overestimates the price of tuition at public institutions. In answering questions about the price of tuition, the average respondent estimate put the price of tuition more than three times higher than the average actual price.[18]

Increases and decreases in tuition, fees, and financial aid may affect student access to college, choice of schools, affordability, and, ultimately, the completion of a degree or certificate program. This section focuses on sticker price. Data on net price are discussed in a subsequent section.

SUBSIDIZING COSTS

The cost of educating college students exceeds the sticker price charged by institutions; that is, in general, those students who pay the full price of their bills out of their own pockets do not pay actually pay the full amount it costs an institution to educate them. Institutions make up the difference between what students pay and the actual cost of providing an education through subsidy payments supported by other sources of revenue, such as state appropriations, endowment earnings, private donations, and federal grants. Both public and private institutions provide some level of subsidy to students.[19]

To illustrate how the subsidy works, assume that the cost of education at a given institution is $10,000.[20] The institution receives $8,000 per student in state appropriations and charges $2,000 in tuition; thus, each student is then facing a tuition level of 20% of the actual cost.[21] Thus, all students, even students who pay the full $2,000 in tuition, are subsidized.

As some researchers have noted, increases in college price do not necessarily mean that costs have increased but could mean that a source of revenue used to support the subsidy has decreased. Returning to the previous example, suppose the next year that the state appropriation per student is reduced to $7,000, while the cost of providing an education remains at $10,000. Tuition is raised to $3,000 to accommodate the change in state appropriations; thus, each student now pays 30% of the actual cost, but tuition has increased by 50%. As discussed elsewhere in this report, the proportion of revenue that institutions derive from tuition and fees has been increasing over time.

In the previous example, the subsidy came simply from state appropriations, which is the largest source of revenue for public institutions. The largest source of funds for subsidizing education costs at private not-for-profit institutions, however, is investment income from endowments and annual donations. Even public institutions are increasingly relying on philanthropic support for operations and capital projects. By contrast, private for-profit institutions are tuition-dependent and, in keeping with their business model, price the education they provide higher than cost in order to make a profit.

In-State Versus Out-of-State Tuition at Public Institutions

The majority of this report focuses on in-state tuition. Students and families' tax dollars support public institutions in the form of appropriation subsidies to state colleges and universities. Public institutions then grant their state residents a greater subsidy, in the form of lower tuition, than is provided to out-of-state students (who have not paid state taxes). Further, state leaders contend that it is in the best interest of the state to educate its residents in order to subsequently realize long-term human capital gains. Thus, to encourage attendance and increase access to higher education for state residents, institutions charge a lower price for in-state residents than for out-of-state residents.

Although out-of-state tuition is higher than that charged to resident students, the differences in these two prices vary from state to state.[22] Several states charge out-of-state students tuition at or near the full cost of instruction. Other states index nonresident tuition to the price charged for resident students. Note that although nonresident students are charged a higher sticker price, they still might be subsidized in other ways. States and institutions often have pricing policies and scholarship aid designed to encourage resident students to stay or to encourage out-of-state students to enroll.

PRICE OF ATTENDANCE

Trends in tuition and required fees point to steady increases in current dollars over the past 30 years (table 3).[23] From 1976-1977 to 2005-2006, tuition at all institutions increased from $924 to $7,601, an increase of 723%. The rate of increase in tuition and fees was higher at four-year institutions, 744%, and lower at two-year institutions, 599%. An examination of institutions by control over the same time period reveals that tuition and fees at public institutions increased more rapidly than tuition and fees at private institutions. Among all public institutions, tuition and fees rose 709% compared with a 665% increase at private institutions.

Figure 1 presents the average sticker price of tuition and required fee charges at the nation's public and private four-year universities[24] from 1964-1995 to 2005-2006. Although college prices have continually increased over the past several decades, the rate of increase is not even. For example, in the 1980s, public four-year universities increased tuition and fee charges by 9.28% annually, on average; for private four-year universities, the average annual increases were 10.53%.[25] By contrast, in the 1990s university price increases slowed down, with public four-year universities raising undergraduate rates by an average of 6.38% annually and private four-year universities by 6.45% annually. In the current decade, rates of increases have begun to climb again for public four-year universities, with tuition and fee prices increasing by an average of 9.26% annually. For private four-year universities in the 2000s, increases have slowed to an average of 5.72% annually.[26]

Table 3. Average Undergraduate Tuition and Fees and Room and Board Paid by Full-Time-Equivalent Students in Degree- Granting Institutions, by Type and Control of Institution: Selected Years, 1976-1977 to 2005-2006 (in current dollars)

Year and Control of Institution	Total Tuition, Fees, Room, and Board			Tuition and Required Fees		
	All Institutions	All Four-Year[a]	Two-Year	All Institutions	All Four-Year[a]	Two-Year
All Institutions (in-state for public institutions)						
1976-1977	2,275	2,577	1,598	924	1,218	346
1981-1982	3,489	3,951	2,476	1,457	1,907	590
1986-1987	5,206	5,964	3,295	2,312	3,042	897
1991-1992	7,077	8,238	4,092	3,286	4,385	1,189
1996-1997	9,206	10,841	4,895	4,564	6,118	1,543
2001-2002	11,380	13,639	5,718	5,646	7,786	1,800
2005-2006	14,629	17,447	7,231	7,601	10,279	2,417
Public Institutions (in state)						
1976-1977	1,789	1,935	1,491	479	617	283
1981-1982	2,663	2,871	2,224	714	909	434
1986-1987	3,805	4,138	2,989	1,106	1,414	660
1991-1992	5,138	5,693	3,623	1,628	2,117	936
1996-1997	6,530	7,334	4,404	2,271	2,987	1,276
2001-2002	8,022	9,196	5,137	2,700	3,735	1,380
2005-2006	10,454	12,108	6,492	3,874	5,351	1,935
Private Institutions						
1976-1977	3,906	3,977	2,971	2,467	2,534	1,592
1981-1982	6,166	6,330	4,746	3,953	4,113	2,605

Table 3. (Continued)

Year and Control of Institution	Total Tuition, Fees, Room, and Board			Tuition and Required Fees		
	All Institutions	All Four-Year[a]	Two-Year	All Institutions	All Four-Year[a]	Two-Year
1986-1987	9,676	10,039	6,384	6,316	6,658	3,684
1991-1992	13,892	14,258	9,632	9,419	9,759	5,754
1996-1997	18,039	18,442	11,954	12,498	12,881	7,236
2001-2002	22,413	22,896	15,825	15,742	16,211	10,076
2005-2006	26,889	27,317	21,170	18,862	19,292	12,450

Source: U.S. Department of Education, National Center for Education Statistics, Digest of Education Statistics 2006, Table 319, at [http://www.nces.ed.gov/].

Note: Data are for the entire academic year and are average charges paid by students. Tuition and fees were weighted by the number of full-time-equivalent undergraduates but were not adjusted to reflect student residency. Room and board were based on full-time students. See source for additional information.

[a]. "All Four-Year" includes universities and other four-year institutions.

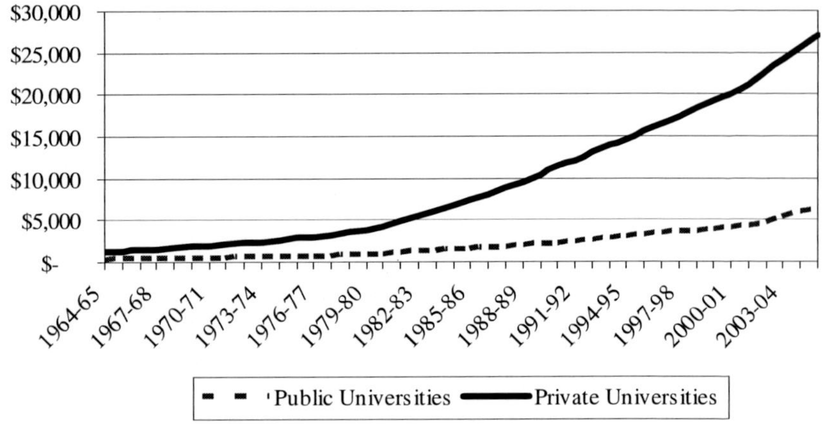

Source: Compiled by CRS on the basis of ED, *Digest 2006*, table 319.

Figure 1. Average 4-Year University Tuition and Required Fee Prices, by Control, 1964-1995 to 2005-2006.

OTHER WAYS OF INTERPRETING PRICE

In addition to simply viewing college prices and changes over time, there are alternate ways of analyzing price. One approach looks at price in relation to overall inflation increases. A second looks at price as a percent of family incomes.

Tuition and Fees Adjusted for Inflation

Examining tuition using current dollars identifies changes in tuition over time but fails to take into account inflationary factors affecting college price. Adjusting college prices for inflation using an index such as the Consumer Price Index for All Urban Consumers (CPI-U)[27] enables direct comparisons in college price to be made across years by adjusting all prices to be comparable with a base year. More simply, adjusting for inflation means that the price of tuition in a given year, such as 1981-1982, has been recalculated to determine what the price of tuition that year would have been in today's dollars.

When increases in tuition are considered in constant dollars (i.e., dollars adjusted for inflation), the increase in tuition over the past 30 years is substantially lower (see Appendix, table A-1). From 1976-1977 to 2005-2006, the tuition increase in constant dollars for all institutions was 140% compared with an increase of 723% in current dollars. Similar differences in increases are evident for four-year, two-year, public, and private institutions. For example, in constant dollars, the increase in tuition at public four-year institutions over this time period was 153% in constant dollars compared with 767% in current dollars.

An alternative method of using inflation to analyze price is to consider whether price increases are outpacing inflation — whether annual percentage increases in tuition exceeds annual percentage increases in the CPI-U. Any such increase that exceeds the inflation rate can be thought of as an increase that "outpaces" inflation. From 1976-1977 to 2005-2006, average tuition at public and private institutions increased by 723%. At four-year institutions, the growth has been even higher, 744%, while it was 599% at two-year colleges. By comparison, the CPI-U grew 243% from 1976 to 2005. By this estimation, four-year college tuition has risen by more than 3 times the rate of inflation over the past 30 years.

Looking more specifically at year-to-year changes, figure 2 shows annual price increases for just one segment of higher education institutions — public four-year universities — in comparison to annual changes in inflation.

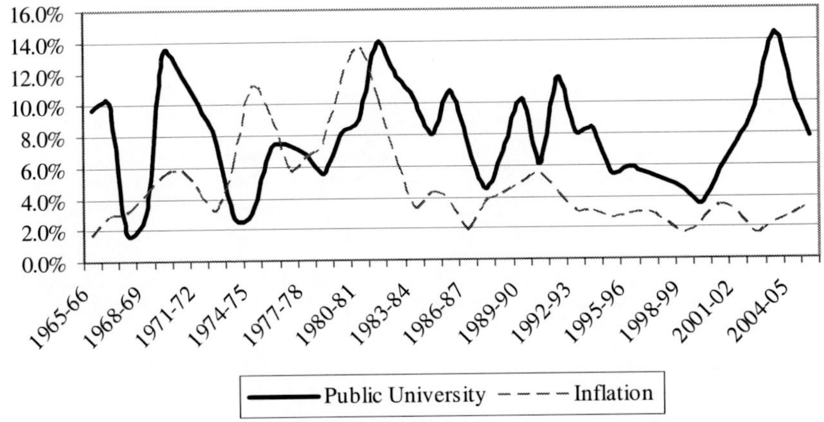

Source: CRS analysis based on average tuition, room, and board charges for all four-year universities (ED, *Digest 2006*, table 319) and inflation as measured by the CPI-U (Bureau of Labor Statistics at [http://www.bls.gov/cpi/#data]).

Figure 2. Annual Percentage Increase, Public Four-Year University Tuition and Required Fees vs. Inflation, 1965-1966 to 2005-2006.

Price as a Share of Family Income

An alternate perspective is to consider college prices as a share of family income. Researchers have found that family incomes have not kept pace with tuition increases — particularly for the lowest-income families.[28] This analysis focuses on overall mean household income and the mean household income of households in the lowest and highest 20% of households according to mean income, as well as households in the middle of this distribution of mean income (i.e., third or middle quintile).

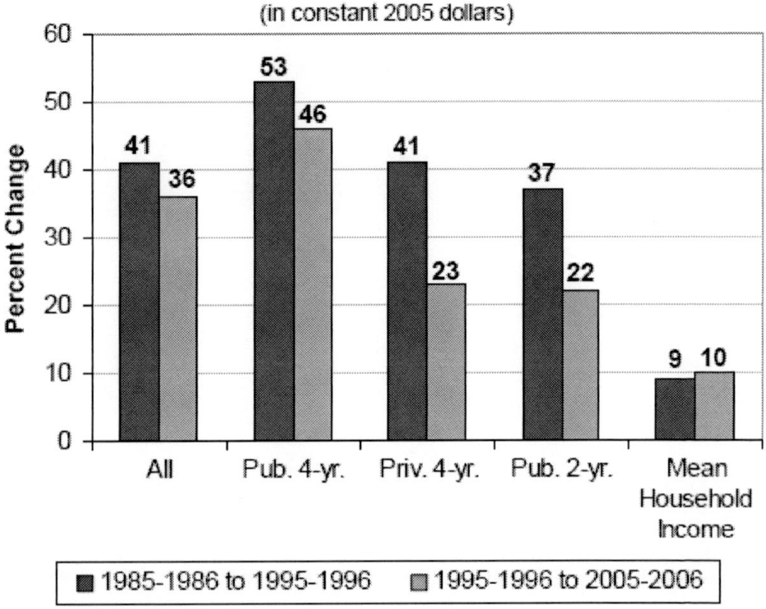

Source: CRS analysis based on U.S. Department of Education, National Center for Education Statistics, *Digest of Education Statistics 2006*, table 319, available at [http://www.nces.ed.gov]; Bureau of Labor Statistics, annual unadjusted Consumer Price Index-Urban (CPI-U) data, available at [http://www.bls.gov]; and U.S. Census Bureau, Historical Income tables — Households, table H-6, available at [http://www.census.gov/hhes/www/income/histinc/h06ar.html].

Note: Percentage changes were calculated based on dollar figures in constant 2005 dollars. Tuition and fees were adjusted for inflation using the annual August CPI-U index to coincide with the start of most academic years. Mean household income was adjusted for inflation using the annual CPI-U index.

Figure 3. Percent Changes in Tuition and Fees and Mean Household Income: 1985-1986 to 1995-1996 and 1995-1996 to 2005-2006.

The share that college prices represent relative to family income has been growing over the past two decades because tuition is increasing faster than income. From the mid-1980s to the mid-1990s, increases in tuition levels averaged across institutions were about four times higher than growth in mean household income. While the discrepancy in growth diminished during the following decade, tuition increases continued to outpace the growth in mean household income, across public and private four-year institutions and public two-year institutions, as shown in figure 3.

When income is analyzed by households using mean income in the top quintile, third quintile (or middle quintile), and lowest quintile, other trends become apparent. From the mid-1980s to the mid1990s, all three groups saw growth in their mean household income outpaced by increases in tuition (figure 4). For households in the lowest quintile, tuition increased at a rate about eight times higher than mean income. For households in the middle quintile, tuition increased at a rate of about 20 times that of mean income. For households in the highest quintile, tuition increased at a rate of about 2.5 times that of mean income. During the following decade, only the middle and highest income groups experienced growth in mean income; the lowest income group had their mean income decline by 0.4%. Similar to the previous decade, the growth in tuition and fees continued to outpace the growth in mean income for all three income groups, but the difference in growth rates was particularly substantial for those in the lowest income group.

As a percentage of income, tuition consumed a larger proportion of mean household income for households in each of the quintiles over time for each of the education options considered in table 4 but consistently consumed a larger share of household income for households in the lowest quintile. For example, the percentage of household income for households in the lowest income quintile needed to pay tuition at public and private four-year and public two-year institutions increased from 38.9% in 1985 to 71.3% in 2005, while increasing from 9.3% to 16.4% for households in the middle quintile and increasing from 3.3% to 4.8% for households in the highest quintile. When only public institutions were considered, the percentage of mean household income needed to pay tuition and fees dropped, particularly for public two-year institutions, but still required a substantially greater proportion of mean household income from households in the lowest quintile than from those in the middle- or higher-income quintiles.

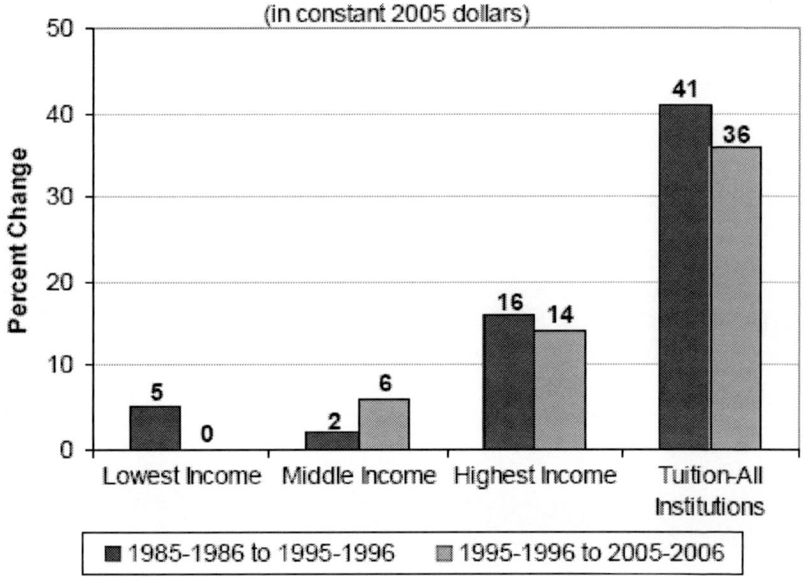

Source: CRS analysis based on U.S. Department of Education, National Center for Education Statistics, *Digest of Education Statistics 2006*, table 319, available at [http://www.nces.ed.gov]; Bureau of Labor Statistics, annual unadjusted Consumer Price Index-Urban (CPI-U) data, available at [http://www.bls.gov]; and U.S. Census Bureau, Historical Income tables — Households, table H-3, available at [http://www.census.gov/hhes/www/income/histinc/h03ar.html].

Note: Percentage changes were calculated based on dollar figures in constant 2005 dollars. Tuition and fees were adjusted for inflation using the annual August CPI-U index to coincide with the start of most academic years. Mean household income was adjusted for inflation using the annual CPI-U index.

Figure 4. Percent Change in Mean Household Income for Households in the Top, Middle, and Bottom Quintiles and Changes in Tuition and Fees: 1995-1986 to 1995-1996 and 1995-1996 to 2005-2006.

These comparisons are based on sticker prices, not net prices. Because many students do not pay the sticker price to attend college, the discrepancies between increases in income and tuition may not be as substantial if net price were considered.[29]

Table 4. Tuition and Fees as a Percentage of Mean Household Income at Public and Private Institutions, by Selected Income Quintile for Selected Years (in Constant 2005 Dollars)

Year and Income Quintile	Mean income	All Public and Private Four-Year and Public Two- Year Institutions		Public Four-Year		Public Two-Year	
		Price	Percent of Mean Income	Price	Percent of Mean Income	Price	Percent of Mean Income
1985 (Mean Income) and 1985-1986 (Tuition and Fees)							
Lowest quintile	$10,190	$3,966	38.9%	$2,397	23.5%	$1,166	11.4%
Middle quintile	$42,863	$3,966	9.3%	$2,397	5.6%	$1,166	2.7%
Highest quintile	$120,434	$3,966	3.3%	$2,397	2.0%	$1,166	1.0%
1995 (Mean Income) and 1995-1996 (Tuition and Fees)							
Lowest quintile	$10,694	$5,572	52.1%	$3,658	34.2%	$1,591	14.9%
Middle quintile	$43,707	$5,572	12.7%	$3,658	8.4%	$1,591	3.6%
Highest quintile	$140,210	$5,572	4.0%	$3,658	2.6%	$1,591	1.1%
2005 (Mean Income) and 2005-2006 (Tuition and Fees)							
Lowest quintile	$10,655	$7,601	71.3%	$5,351	50.2%	$1,935	18.2%
Middle quintile	$46,301	$7,601	16.4%	$5,351	11.6%	$1,935	4.2%
Highest quintile	$159,583	$7,601	4.8%	$5,351	3.4%	$1,935	1.2%

Source: CRS analysis based on U.S. Department of Education, National Center for Education Statistics, *Digest of Education Statistics 2006*, Table 319, available at [http://www.nces.ed.gov]; Bureau of Labor Statistics, annual unadjusted Consumer Price Index-Urban (CPI-U) data, available at [http://www.bls.gov]; and U.S. Census Bureau, Historical Income tables — Households, table H-6, available at [http://www.census.gov/ hhes/www/income/histinc/h03ar.html].

Note: Percentage changes were calculated on the basis of dollar figures in constant 2005 dollars. Tuition and fees were adjusted for inflation using the annual August CPI-U index to coincide with the start of most academic years. Mean household income was adjusted for inflation using the annual CPI-U index.

Table 5. Average Undergraduate Tuition, Fees, Room, and Board Charged for Full-Time Students in Degree-Granting Institutions, by Type and Control of Institution and State: 2005-2006

State	Public Four-Year			Private Four-Year			Public Two-Year
	Total	Tuition and Required Fees (in- state)	Room and Board	Total	Tuition and Required Fees (in- state)	Room and Board	Tuition and Required Fees (in- state)
United States	12,108	5,351	6,757	27,317	19,292	8,025	1,935
Alabama	9,625	4,578	5,047	18,520	12,426	6,094	2,764
Alaska	10,620	4,054	6,566	21,651	14,891	6,760	2,353
Arizona	11,480	4,426	7,054	18,734	11,397	7,336	1,344
Arkansas	9,192	4,643	4,549	18,122	12,691	5,431	1,780
California	13,685	4,408	9,277	31,266	21,691	9,575	718
Colorado	11,569	4,465	7,104	27,779	18,493	9,286	1,991
Connecticut	14,658	6,709	7,949	36,026	26,183	9,843	2,536
Delaware	14,326	7,074	7,253	18,176	10,819	7,357	2,240
District of Columbia	na	2,070	na	32,556	22,748	9,808	na
Florida	10,141	2,941	7,200	24,985	17,503	7,482	1,844
Georgia	10,062	3,632	6,430	26,081	18,120	7,961	1,645
Hawaii	9,042	3,226	5,816	19,437	10,334	9,103	1,226
Idaho	8,982	3,919	5,063	11,614	5,490	6,125	1,891
Illinois	13,976	7,158	6,818	27,875	19,406	8,469	2,104
Indiana	12,388	5,892	6,497	27,582	20,851	6,731	2,589
Iowa	12,329	5,619	6,710	23,444	17,513	5,932	3,032
Kansas	9,980	4,560	5,421	20,741	15,044	5,697	1,938
Kentucky	10,663	5,136	5,527	20,674	13,764	6,910	2,404
Louisiana	8,506	3,679	4,827	17,207	11,264	5,944	1,469

Table 5. (Continued)

State	Public Four-Year			Private Four-Year			Public Two-Year
	Total	Tuition and Required Fees (in- state)	Room and Board	Total	Tuition and Required Fees (in- state)	Room and Board	Tuition and Required Fees (in- state)
Maine	12,568	6,027	6,541	29,550	21,508	8,042	3,039
Maryland	14,793	7,045	7,747	32,617	23,934	8,682	2,833
Massachusetts	14,651	7,290	7,361	37,282	27,335	9,947	2,925
Michigan	13,693	6,938	6,756	19,732	13,303	6,429	2,076
Minnesota	12,777	6,912	5,865	27,314	20,519	6,795	4,085
Mississippi	9,461	4,177	5,284	17,112	11,839	5,273	1,660
Missouri	11,861	5,831	6,030	22,441	15,718	6,722	2,247
Montana	10,613	4,952	5,661	18,093	12,937	5,156	2,721
Nebraska	11,286	4,880	6,406	21,017	15,234	5,782	1,899
Nevada	10,865	2,671	8,194	20,691	12,622	8,069	1,635
New Hampshire	15,479	8,458	7,021	31,154	22,534	8,620	5,720
New Jersey	17,708	8,649	9,059	31,335	22,114	9,221	2,712
New Mexico	9,579	3,701	5,878	20,006	13,256	6,750	1,179
New York	13,275	4,987	8,288	32,478	22,900	9,579	3,181
North Carolina	9,675	3,631	6,044	26,411	19,166	7,245	1,295
North Dakota	9,829	5,038	4,791	13,553	9,376	4,177	3,084
Ohio	16,032	8,457	7,576	26,906	19,901	7,006	3,127
Oklahoma	9,404	3,806	5,598	20,113	14,033	6,080	2,111
Oregon	12,720	5,348	7,373	27,945	20,844	7,101	2,635
Pennsylvania	15,464	8,710	6,754	31,963	23,450	8,514	2,976
Rhode Island	14,315	6,316	7,998	33,101	24,140	8,960	2,470

Table 5. (Continued)

State	Public Four-Year			Private Four-Year			Public Two-Year
	Total	Tuition and Required Fees (in- state)	Room and Board	Total	Tuition and Required Fees (in- state)	Room and Board	Tuition and Required Fees (in- state)
South Carolina	13,145	7,337	5,808	22,170	16,165	6,005	2,932
South Dakota	9,493	4,908	4,585	18,930	13,686	5,245	3,154
Tennessee	9,956	4,765	5,190	23,039	16,552	6,488	2,395
Texas	10,973	4,666	6,307	23,440	16,809	6,630	1,273
Utah	8,745	3,445	5,300	11,275	5,249	6,026	2,224
Vermont	16,571	9,279	7,292	29,072	21,273	7,799	4,012
Virginia	12,279	5,912	6,367	23,823	17,185	6,637	2,049
Washington	12,384	5,250	7,135	27,280	20,110	7,170	2,554
West Virginia	9,992	3,816	6,176	20,002	13,856	6,147	2,509
Wisconsin	10,560	5,672	4,888	25,656	19,083	6,574	2,965
Wyoming	8,946	2,874	6,072	na	9,450	na	1,772

Source: Table prepared by CRS based on data available from the U.S. Department of Education, National Center for Education Statistics, *Digest of Education Statistics, 2006*, table 320.

Note: Data are for the entire academic year and are average charges. Tuition and fees were weighted by the number of full-time-equivalent undergraduates, but were not adjusted to reflect student residency. Room and board are based on full-time students. Degree-granting institutions grant associate's or higher degrees and participate in Title IV federal financial aid programs. Private four-year institutions include both non-profit and for-profit institutions. For additional information about the data, see the source noted above.

PRICES BY STATE

This section provides a brief overview of the price of higher education across the 50 states and the District of Columbia during the 2005-2006 academic year. As shown on table 5, the average tuition, fees, room, and board charged for full-time students attending public four-year degree-granting institutions was $12,108. The average tuition, fees, room, and board at private (non-profit and for-profit) four-year degree-granting institutions was more than twice this amount. The difference in average tuition, fees, room, and board charged by public and private four-year degree-granting institutions was driven primarily by differences in average tuition and required fees ($5,351 versus $19,292, respectively), as the difference in average room and board between public and private four-year degree-grant institutions was about $1,300. The average tuition and fees at public two-year degree-granting institutions was just under $2,000. In just over half the states, average tuition and fees at public two-year institutions were less than or equal to 50% of the average tuition and fees at public four-year institutions in the same state.

Chapter 4

NET PRICE OF A COLLEGE EDUCATION

After considering the cost of a college and the price students are initially asked to pay, a third measure of college expenses is *net price*. Net price is a measure of price that takes into account financial aid provided to students. It is the actual price students and their families need to pay out of their own pockets to attend college.

Student aid for postsecondary education may be need-based aid or merit-based aid. Need-based aid addresses concerns of access and affordability through grants and loans, while merit-based aid programs are designed to recognize student achievement through tuition waivers and scholarships. Numerous entities provide student aid, including states, local governments, institutions, foundations, and the federal government.

In 2006-2007, over $149.0 billion was awarded in student aid from all sources.[30] About 58% of this amount was generated by the federal government through appropriations, loan guarantees, and tax credits. For the federal government, providing access to postsecondary education for low-income students has been the focus of student aid programs. Federal grant aid from all programs totaled $19.6 billion in the last academic year, while federally backed loan disbursements totaled $59.6 billion. From federal, state, institutional, and private sources, grant aid to students — which does not have to be repaid and therefore lowers out-of-pocket payments — totaled $63.9 billion.

Total federal aid has grown 128% over the past ten years (starting from $37.9 billion). However, its overall proportion of student aid is falling: in 1996-1997, federal aid represented 66% of all aid, compared with about 58% in 2006-2007. State, institutional, and private aid have been outpacing federal aid growth over the past decade, with private grants growing by 206% and private loans growing by 989%.[31]

Although student financial aid from non-federal sources contributes substantially to lowering net price, the focus of this section is on federal student aid programs and their role in lowering out-of-pocket expenses for students. The two largest federal aid programs, Pell Grants and federal student loans, are authorized under Title IV of the HEA. The third largest (measured in terms of aid provided) source of financial assistance is federal income tax-related credits, deductions, and benefits.[32]

FEDERAL FINANCIAL AID

The federal government currently provides several forms of support to help students pursue a postsecondary education. This aid takes the form of grants, loans, tax credits, tax deductions, and tax-favored education savings benefits.[33] Pell Grants and federal student loans are the two largest federal aid programs.[34]

Pell Grants[35]

The Pell Grant program, authorized by Title IV of the HEA, is the single largest source of grant aid for postsecondary education provided by the federal government. Pell Grants are need-based aid intended to be the foundation for all federal student aid awarded to undergraduate students. There is no absolute income threshold that determines program eligibility, but most Pell Grant recipients are low-income students. For FY2006, it is estimated that the program provided nearly $13 billion to about 5.4 million undergraduate students. For FY2007, the maximum Pell Grant award was $4,310.

Loan Programs[36]

The federal government operates two major student loan programs: the Federal Family Education Loan (FFEL) program, authorized by Part B of Title IV of the HEA; and the William D. Ford Direct Loan (DL) program, authorized by Part D of Title IV of the HEA. These programs provide loans to undergraduate and graduate students and the parents of undergraduate students to help them meet the costs of postsecondary education. The FFEL and DL programs provide more direct aid to students pursuing postsecondary education than any other single source. The loans made through these programs are low-interest loans. In FY2005, these programs provided $56.2 billion in new loans to students and their parents.

Loans made through the FFEL and DL programs are provided to students pursuing a postsecondary education on at least a half-time basis at eligible postsecondary institutions. Student borrowers receiving loans through these programs are able to postpone loan repayment until they complete their academic programs and may also defer payment to pursue additional postsecondary studies.

STUDENTS RECEIVING AID

In 2003-2004, about 76% of all full-time, full-year undergraduates received some form of financial aid (table 6). The percentage of students receiving any *federal* aid varied by control of institution, ranging from 56% of students at public institutions to 87% of students at private for-profit institutions. Over two-fifths (41%) of full-time, full-year undergraduates attending public institutions received federal loans. Higher percentages of students received federal loans at private institutions, with 64% of students at private not-for-profit institutions and 78% of students at private for-profit institutions receiving federal loans. Nearly a quarter of full-time, full-year undergraduates at private not-for-profit colleges received federal work study, but far fewer students did so at other types of institutions.

Surprisingly similar percentages of students in different income groups received financial aid in 2003-2004. Nearly 63% of dependent undergraduates from families earning less than $20,000 per year received some form of aid, while approximately 61% of students from families earning over $100,000 did so.[37] However, the distribution of aid by income group varies significantly by type of aid. For example, over 32% of dependent undergraduates in the lowest income group were awarded federal grant aid, while these awards went to 1% of dependent undergraduates in the highest income group.

Reliance on loans to finance higher education is increasing. In 1996-1997, students and their parents took out nearly $28.8 billion in federal student loans. By 2006-2007, students and families are expected to borrow approximately $59.6 billion in federal student loans — more than doubling in 10 years.[38]

Table 6. Percentage of Full-Time, Full-Year Undergraduates Receiving Aid, by Source and Type of Aid and Control of Institution: 2003-2004

Control of Institution	Percentage of Students Receiving Aid by Source of Aid				
	Any Aid	Any Federal	Federal Grants	Federal Loans	Federal Work Study
All	76.1%	61.7%	33.2%	48.5%	10.3%
Public	71.1	56.1	31.6	41.1	7.3
Private Not- For-Profit	88.6	73.1	31.9	64.4	23.0
Private For- Profit	92.1	86.9	54.8	78.2	3.1

Source: U.S. Department of Education, National Center for Education Statistics. *Digest of Education Statistics: 2006*, Table 327. Data drawn from National Postsecondary Student Aid Study (NPSAS), 2004, at [http://www.nces.ed.gov/].

NET PRICE AFTER GRANTS

A recent study of college price and financial aid awards for 2003-2004 examined the issue of net price by type of institution.[39] Defining *net price* as total price of attendance minus *grant aid*, the average net price for all students (including those not receiving any grant aid) was as follows: at public two-year colleges, $8,700; at public four-year institutions, $12,400; at private not-for-profit four-year institutions, $17,400; and at private for-profit institutions, $20,600.[40] For low-income families of dependent undergraduates (whose incomes are in the bottom quartile of families, earning less than $32,000), net price was lower: at public two-year colleges, $6,700; at public four-year institutions, $9,000; at private not-for-profit four-year institutions, $15,500; and at private for-profit institutions, $15,700.

Chapter 5

INFLUENCES ON COLLEGE COSTS AND PRICES

Researchers have been studying the issue of tuition increases for many years. On the basis of their work, it has been determined that the price of postsecondary education is established in multiple ways and differs for public and private institutions. Because of limitations in the data, however, it has been difficult to determine specific internal and external factors that have a strong relationship with price increases.

INFLUENCES ON COSTS

Researchers have studied whether institutional costs, that is, trends in the cost of items for which colleges and universities pay, drive increases in price. Current analysis suggests that there is not a strong relationship between costs colleges incur and price.[41] Although evidence does not point to a strong relationship, it could be argued that revenue must cover or exceed institutional costs or an institution may go into debt. Researchers have determined, however, that most postsecondary institutions do not function like businesses (with the notable exception of for-profit colleges). The labor-intensive nature of providing a higher education makes it difficult to realize productivity gains. For example, increasing class sizes to reduce costs might result in a decline in quality rather than an increase in productivity.[42]

Researchers have identified various factors that drive institutional costs. For example, a recent summary of relevant literature identified five primary cost drivers: (1) revenue availability; (2) institutional aid; (3) mission and discipline; (4) faculty compensation and workload policies; and (5) class size.[43] Other researchers have pointed to specific costs that institutions are facing, including the provision of technology, increasing health care costs, burdens associated with government regulation, facilities, enrollment, and student expectations.[44]

More specifically, for example, the mission and discipline of an institution can have substantial cost ramifications, as institutions with research programs, graduate education, and public service missions have higher costs than other institutions.[45] These costs may be even higher if the institution offers engineering or other science programs with laboratory components. Providing students, faculty, and staff with access to technology incurs infrastructure costs, as well as costs associated with continual updating of hardware, software, and connections. Some institutions have imposed new technology fees to have students cover some of these costs.

ESTABLISHING PRICE AT PUBLIC INSTITUTIONS

States differ in the basic philosophy that guides their decision making with respect to setting tuition levels for public institutions. The majority of states have embraced a philosophy of low tuition to maximize access to postsecondary education by making it as affordable as possible.[46] States that have adopted a philosophy on the basis of higher levels of tuition, on the other hand, often provide substantial student financial aid to help ensure access for low-income students.

Primary authority to establish tuition levels may rest with the legislature, state coordinating or governing agency, individual system boards, or individual institutions. In 13 states, the state coordinating/governing agency has the primary authority to establish tuition levels. Fourteen states delegate this power to individual institutions with varying levels of discretion, while 26 states rely on individual system or local district boards. Five states give primary tuition-setting authority to the state legislature.[47]

According to states, when setting in-state tuition, state general fund appropriations have the most significant influence on this decision.[48] For most states, there are no formal incentives to limit tuition increases, but many operate under informal incentives, such as the desire to provide an affordable education.[49] States or institutions also may opt to place self-imposed limitations on tuition increases.[50] For example, a State Higher Education Executive Officers study found that 18 states had applied some type of limitation on tuition increases during the previous three fiscal years, including capping tuition increases at a certain percentage, freezing tuition at a specific level, or indexing tuition to a measure of inflation.

An NCES-commissioned study examining college costs and price provides some evidence as to factors that may be related to tuition increases. The specific factors differ according to the level and control of the institution. At public four-year institutions, a decline in state appropriations revenue was found to be the most important factor associated with changes in tuition. According to the Institute for Higher Education Policy (IHEP), the increase in price results from institutions attempting to maintain their total revenue when state appropriations decline.[51] An increase in instructional expenditures also was associated with changes in tuition, but the relationship was not as strong. At public two-year institutions, changes in revenues, including state appropriations, and expenditures accounted for only a small proportion of changes in tuition. This is attributed to overriding efforts by public two-year institutions to maintain relatively low tuition. These institutions often will opt to make other changes, such as reducing courses, eliminating programs, or reducing services before they will increase price. Thus, tuition changes at public two-year and public four-year institutions are affected by different factors.

State Support

For FY2006, state tax funds appropriated for higher education operating expenses (e.g., colleges and universities, student aid, governing boards) totaled $67.2 billion.[52] This represented an overall increase of 7.1% in appropriated funds from the previous year and a 14.4% increase in appropriated funds from FY2004. Looking at trends over time, from FY1996 to FY2006, overall state appropriations increased 54.7%, with increases in appropriations occurring in every state for which data were available.[53]

When states contend with serious financial difficulties, resulting in smaller increases in support for higher education than in previous years or outright reductions in support for higher education, public institutions are affected by these decisions. A substantial decline in state appropriations, especially at four-year institutions, may lead to large percentage or dollar increases in tuition (or both), regardless of whether the actual cost of providing the education also increases. In addition, as enrollment in higher education continues to increase, per student appropriations may be reduced if corresponding increases are not made in state appropriations for higher education.

Research has shown that changes in revenues and expenditures do not have as substantial an effect on tuition at public two-year institutions. These institutions may maintain current tuition levels or eliminate the need for large tuition increases by reducing course offerings, services, or enrollment. These types of changes ultimately may be restricting access to postsecondary education, as there may be fewer seats or services available. This could be particularly troublesome for low-income students, non-traditional students, and individuals seeking to return to school for additional training.

Decreases in state appropriations may also mean less money is available to support institutional aid, which may, in turn, reduce student access to postsecondary education. For example, institutions that rely on state appropriations to offer institutional aid may find that they need to shift money that would have been used to provide aid to other purposes. They might use available state appropriations to affect tuition levels rather than using state appropriations to support student aid. Although this practice may be beneficial to all students in terms of the price of college, low-income students dependent on institutional aid may no longer receive needed support.

ESTABLISHING PRICE AT PRIVATE INSTITUTIONS

In a discussion of primarily non-public institutions, IHEP divides the non-public sector into three markets: (1) highly selective institutions — predominantly private not-for-profit institutions, as well as a few highly selective public institutions; (2) competitive institutions; and (3) proprietary institutions.[54] Highly selective institutions are primarily private not-for-profit institutions that experience excess demand for their available openings. These institutions tend to compete against one another on the basis of non-price mechanisms, such as institutional reputation. They generally have similar prices and often have higher levels of institutional wealth than other types of institutions.[55]

Competitive institutions also compete with their peer institutions but on a regional rather than national level. They tend to compete through non-price mechanisms and tuition discounting for specific groups of students. Prices within a specific group of peer institutions tend to cluster in a narrow range.

Less is known about proprietary institutions. However, by definition, these for-profit institutions exist to make a profit. As previously discussed, tuition is their primary source of revenue, so the costs of educating students at these institutions may be more closely related to price than at other types of institutions.

The NCES study examining college costs and prices found that factors affecting tuition at private not-for-profit four-year institutions are more varied.[56] That is, unlike public four-year institutions, no single factor is strongly related to tuition changes. Rather, prices at private not-for-profit four-year institutions are driven by internal institutional budget controls and external market conditions. Among the internal factors associated with higher tuition were higher costs for institutional aid and faculty salaries and declining revenues from endowments and private giving. Among the external factors associated with tuition changes were the availability of institutional aid, price of public institutions in the same state, and per capita income in the state.

Tuition Discounting and Net Price

Tuition discounting is a practice by which institutions charge students less than the sticker price. This is intended to increase net revenue, attract minority students, increase enrollment, or attract academically talented students.[57] It is unclear whether this strategy ultimately accomplishes these goals. For example, one question focuses on whether reductions in tuition provided for students who are able to pay based on formulas such as the Expected Family Contribution (EFC), but are unwilling to pay the sticker price, results in enrollment in the institution that otherwise would not have occurred, potentially contributing to net revenue. Another issue focuses on whether by subsidizing students able to pay to attend college, funds are being diverted from needy students or from improvements in academic programs or services. A third issue focuses on whether the practice of tuition discounting causes institutions to raise prices, knowing that many students will not pay the full sticker price ultimately. Last, the question remains whether an alternative strategy of across-the-board reductions in price to the level at which tuition is generally discounted would result in increased enrollment, increased net revenue, or recruitment of the desired student body.

A recent study conducted by the Lumina Foundation examined the use of tuition discounting.[58] Researchers state that the practice does work successfully at some institutions but that, when institutional aid practices are examined across all institutions, tuition discounting has some adverse financial effects on low-income students in terms of accessibility and affordability. For example, researchers suggest that if institutions use financial resources to attract students that could afford to pay to attend, then institutions had fewer funds to provide institutional support to low-income students. Researchers support this argument on the basis of data from the National Postsecondary Student Aid Study, which show that between 1995-1996 and 2000-2001, institutional grant aid for higher-income undergraduates rose more quickly than for lower-income undergraduates at four-year institutions. The Lumina Foundation study also found that the use of tuition discounting does not always produce the desired result of increased net revenue, nor does it necessarily lead to the recruitment of the most academically talented students based on the median SAT scores of the students attending institutions using tuition discounting.

Federal Policy Effects on College Price

In analyzing college prices, researchers have considered whether a relationship exists between federal aid and price increases. Although federal grant aid does not seem to affect college prices directly, less is known about the effects of federal loans and tax credits. A direct relationship between loans and higher tuition has not been identified, but an indirect relationship may exist. With respect to tax credits, limited evidence suggests that a relationship may exist under certain circumstances.

Federal Financial Aid and Sticker Price

Federal student aid takes many forms, including grants, loans, and education tax credits. Concerns have been raised by researchers, interest groups, and some Members of Congress about whether increased federal aid contributes to increasing college price. Debate about whether federal financial aid provides incentives for tuition increases was widespread in the 1980s.[59] By the 1990s, much of the debate had narrowed to focus on the relationship, if any, between federal loan aid and price.

Students apply for federal grants and loans using the Free Application for Federal Student Aid (FAFSA) form. Based on information reported on the FAFSA, ED calculates the EFC. In general, most institutions use the EFC to determine students' financial need by determining the difference between the price of attendance and the EFC. Since this calculation takes the price of attendance into account, a direct relationship between federal aid and price only would be likely if increased financial need resulted in increased federal aid. However, federal grant and loan aid are capped at specific amounts.[60] These amounts generally are lower than the price of attendance at many institutions. Thus, an incentive for institutions to increase their price in anticipation of students receiving additional financial aid may exist for institutions with relatively low prices, but it is not as clear that this is so at institutions whose price already exceeds available federal aid.[61]

According to one of the major recent reviews of research, in general, research has shown that no relationship exists between federal grants and college prices.[62] Research on the relationship between federal student loans and tuition, however, has been less conclusive, with some researchers believing that there may be an indirect relationship between federal student loans and college price. For example, institutions may raise prices knowing that students can apply for loans to cover tuition increases. Institutions then may use revenue from tuition increases to provide additional institutional aid to make it possible for some students to access and afford the price of college. At the same time, increased loan availability could reduce the need for institutions to increase price to generate revenue to provide institutional aid because students can receive aid in the form of loans. Thus, it is difficult to determine whether federal student loan programs are contributing to tuition increases.

In its examination of college costs and prices, NCES found virtually no associations between price and most student aid variables, including federal grants and loans, and tuition. The only association that was identified was that institutional aid had a positive association with tuition increases at comprehensive public institutions and comprehensive private not-for-profit institutions.[63] This could be related to institutions increasing tuition to increase revenue to provide institutional aid to students. Thus, in the NCES study, federal grants and loans were not found to have a positive relationship with tuition increases.

Federal Tax Legislation and Sticker Price

Limited data are available about the effect of federal tax credits on tuition increases.[64] A recent Government Accountability Office study concluded that data and methodological challenges make it difficult to identify and isolate the effects of tax credits, as well as grants and loans, on attendance, choice, completion, or costs.[65]

In a recent survey of state higher education agencies, few states reported raising tuition in response to new tax credits or taking federal tax credits into account when calculating student aid eligibility.[66] Most states reported taking advantage of opportunities to create a tax-advantaged state prepayment or college savings plan, and many states indicated they publicize the availability of federal tax credits to help finance college.

However, an analysis of the effect of tax credits on state support for higher education and changes in college prices found that a relationship does exist between tax credits and state appropriations and tax credits and price under certain circumstances.[67] For example, the study found that when other factors were held constant, state appropriations to public two-year institutions charging less than $2,000 fell relative to other institutions after the introduction of tax credits. At the same time, states that had developed a track record of supporting student aid programs continued to support, and possibly bolster, these programs despite the availability of additional federal aid.

At the institution level, incentives existed for institutions to increase their prices for students who benefitted from the tax credits; that is, the tax credits increased student income, providing students with more money to pay for college. Evidence indicates that public two-year colleges raised prices higher than what could be explained by fluctuations in state appropriations, and the increases were greater at schools with higher percentages of tax credit-eligible students.[68]

Actions at the State and Institutional Levels

Congress may include provisions related to college costs and prices in HEA reauthorization legislation, but there are also steps to increase affordability that could be taken or are being taken by states and institutions that could either complement federal actions or minimize the need for federal action in some areas.[69] This section provides several examples of strategies currently being implemented by states and institutions to address issues of college costs and price. More specifically, the overview focuses on three key areas: (1) tuition and fees, (2) reducing costs, and (3) college credits.

Tuition and Fees

States and institutions have taken a variety of approaches to making college more affordable for students. For example, Harvard University and the University of Virginia have eliminated tuition and fees for students whose family incomes fall below a specified level.[70] Colorado implemented a voucher system that provides directs stipends to students for tuition payments.[71] Arizona, Mississippi, and New York are considering or implementing tuition policies that link tuition increases to increases in measures of inflation.[72] For example, the former chancellor at the State University of New York (SUNY) proposed tying tuition increases to the Higher Education Price Index (HEPI, discussed below). Other states have proposed freezing tuition and fees at a certain level for a specific number of years. For example, Illinois implemented a strategy to keep tuition at a constant level for four years for each entering class beginning fall 2004,[73] and similar policies are being or have been considered in other states, such as Kansas, Texas, and Indiana.[74] Under a policy that locks in tuition, the tuition charged to a cohort of freshman students will remain constant for four years or more. This enables families to plan for the price of college, essentially making a payment for a college education similar to a mortgage payment that can be anticipated monthly. Questions have been raised about tuition freeze proposals, including concerns that there will be substantial differences in the price charged from one cohort to another.

Reducing Costs

Many states and institutions have already taken the initiative to reduce costs.[75] For example with respect to health care, institutions have formed their own health-care consortia; linked employee contributions to health care costs to salary, meaning that staff members with higher salaries pay more; and focused on employee wellness to achieve costs savings.[76] Other institutions have focused on finding cost savings by sharing other services. For example, five colleges in Massachusetts built their own fiber-optic network rather than paying high fees for broadband Internet service.[77] Institutions in Wisconsin formed a consortia to share office functions while enhancing services at a reduced cost.[78]

Some institutions have accepted greater financial risks in exchange for likely long-term savings.[79] For example, institutions are raising insurance deductibles and altering borrowing strategies to get better interest rates while assuming more risk. Others are considering energy efficiency in their building designs and renovations to achieve long-term savings.[80]

A more widespread cost-saving initiative is to replace tenured, full-time faculty with lower-paid, part-time faculty.[81] Some institutions have instituted differential tuition levels, whereby students in more expensive programs (e.g., engineering) are charged a higher tuition. Institutions are also outsourcing services.[82] Although this has been done for a number of years with respect to bookstores and food services, institutions have now started to outsource facility management, on-campus housing, payroll, and printing.[83]

College Credits

One of the major areas in which states and institutions are focusing their efforts to reduce college costs and the total price of college attendance is with respect to enabling students to earn college credits prior to college attendance and ensuring that credits earned at one institution will be accepted at another institution. According to data collected by the Education Commission of the States (ECS), dual enrollment policies have been implemented through state statute, board policy, or institutional agreement in 47 states.[84] These policies enable high school students to earn college credits while in high school. Many institutions also award students credits on the basis of the completion of Advanced Placement (AP) courses and specific levels of performance on the AP tests. Some institutions also provide students with college credit for completion of an International Baccalaureate (IB) diploma and specific levels of performance on the related tests. Texas recently implemented a law that provides students graduating from a Texas high school with an IB diploma and specific scores on the IB exams with at least 24 semester credits upon enrollment in a Texas public IHE.[85]

All states have some type of agreement with respect to the transfer of credit.[86] These agreements may be established by legislation or created voluntarily on a course-by-course, department-to-department, or institution-to-institution basis. Often these agreements are created between two-year institutions and four-year institutions to facilitate the transfer of credit as students move from one type of institution to the next. They may also exist solely among four-year institutions, two-year institutions, a group of institutions, or just two institutions. The more extensive the agreement in terms of the number of institutions included, the greater the benefit to the student. Some states have enhanced their articulation agreements by establishing a set of general education core curriculum requirements. A general education core curriculum generally refers to a set of courses that fulfill lower-division general education requirements at all institutions participating in the core curriculum system. Some states have adopted common general education courses, while others have identified blocks of courses that are guaranteed to transfer from one institution to another. Overall, 37 states have general education common core courses that transfer from one institution to another under specific circumstances.[87] The completion of these requirements often carries some type of benefit, such as transferring from a two-year institution into a four-year institution with junior status. Nine states have also developed common course numbering.[88] Having common course numbers at two-year and four-year institutions makes it more likely that students will enroll in courses that will ultimately transfer from one institution to another.[89]

Chapter 6

ISSUES FOR THE HIGHER EDUCATION ACT REAUTHORIZATION

Work on the reauthorization of the HEA began during the 108th Congress and has continued through the 110th Congress. During this time, Congress has held numerous hearings on and introduced and passed bills addressing affordability and accessibility issues. Clearly there are concerns about students' and their families' ability to afford college and, consequently, their ability to access postsecondary education opportunities. Congressional involvement with the issue of college price has historically been limited, focusing on issues of access. This raises the question of what the appropriate federal role is, if any, in relation to college prices. Concomitantly, a second question of whether Congress has tools at its disposal that will effectively address issues of college price and cost can be asked. A key issue is how to develop and implement effectively a federal policy related to college price given the diversity of institutions, policies, and price drivers affecting those institutions nationwide.[90] Regardless of the approach ultimately selected, Congress faces the need to balance concerns about affordability and access with the goal of maintaining a high quality system of postsecondary education.

PRICE INDICES

Traditionally, Congress has not embraced a policy role with respect to the prices charged by public and private institutions, choosing instead to address issues of access and affordability from the student financial aid perspective. However, proposals for indexing increases in college price to some measure have been introduced in the 108th, 109th, and 110th Congresses.[91] For example, proposals have been introduced that would compare an institution's percentage increase in tuition and fees against two times the increase in the Consumer Price Index-All Urban Consumers (CPI-U), and require institutions whose percentage increase in tuition and fees exceeded two times the increase in the CPI-U to submit to additional reporting requirements or other penalties. Congressional debate may continue to focus on the use of price indices as a means to temper anticipated increases in tuition.

When considering the implementation of a price index requirement, perhaps the most obvious issue is what to select as the measure to which tuition and fees will be indexed. Three options have been considered in recent years. The first is the CPI-U, produced by the Bureau of Labor Statistics (BLS). The CPI-U is a measure of changes in the price of a market basket of goods and services purchased for consumption by all urban consumers.[92] BLS also produces indices that make it possible to examine changes in the price of college textbooks and college tuition and fees, although these items have not been included in a single index.[93]

A second measure that has been discussed is the Higher Education Price Index (HEPI).[94] The HEPI was created in 1961 by Dr. Kent Halstead and was first published by the U.S. Department of Education in 1975. Since 2005, the HEPI has been managed by the Commonfund Institute.[95] According to the Commonfund, the "HEPI measures the average relative level in the prices of a fixed market basket of goods and services purchased by colleges and universities through current fund educational and general expenditures excluding expenditures for research."[96] The HEPI is calculated using a regression formula that includes professional salaries (e.g, faculty and administrative salaries), nonprofessional wages and salaries (e.g., clerical salaries), fringe benefits, contracted services, supplies and materials, and utilities.[97] It functions as a tool to examine the purchasing power of colleges and universities. That is, by reporting only price changes, without quality or quantity changes, the index essentially tells institutions how much it will cost to maintain the status quo.

Although there are several differences between the CPI-U and the HEPI, two in particular are worth considering. First, as previously discussed, most spending by colleges and universities is for personnel, primarily faculty. Salary increases for postsecondary education personnel are different from those included in the CPI-U, which includes urban wage earners and salaried clerical workers. In addition, the HEPI focuses specifically on goods and services purchased by colleges and universities, while the CPI-U also includes housing, transportation, medical care, and other items. While the CPI-U does have a separate index for tuition and fees, for example, this index has not been considered for use in HEA reauthorization bills that have been reported out of committee in recent years.

Finally, the third index option that has been considered is to create indices using a market basket of higher education goods and services, possibly having a different index for different types of institution on the basis of level and control. It is unclear exactly how this type of index would be different from the HEPI, for example, except that the indices may be designed to further account for distinctions among different types of institutions.

A second difficulty associated with using price indices is related to differences between (1) percentage increases in price and (2) dollar increases in price. If a certain percentage increase is set as a limit in price increases, institutions with relatively low tuition may be penalized for making small changes in the actual dollar amount being charged to students, while institutions with already high tuition levels may be able to make relatively small percentage increases resulting in relatively large dollar increases without penalty. Similar problems could arise from establishing a specific dollar increase as a price increase limit. One possible way to address these problems, in part, would be to establish an index by which to evaluate percentage increases in tuition and fees, while including an exception for institutions for whom violation of the established requirement is associated with a relatively small dollar increase in tuition and fees. Another issue to consider is that, depending on the implementation timeline of such a policy, in the years just prior to the policy taking place, institutions nationwide may seize on their last opportunities to have relatively large tuition and fee increases (in dollars, percentages, or both) without being subject to penalties.

CONTROLLING COLLEGE COSTS

College costs, as previously discussed, refer to what institutions actually expend to educate students. In examining ways to reduce price increases experienced by students, some attention has been given to reducing college costs as a means to reduce the need for institutions to increase their prices. One problem with this approach is the subsidy that students at public and non-profit institutions receive —even students paying the sticker price to attend college are not paying what it actually costs institutions to educate them. Therefore, it is possible that institutions may raise their prices to reduce the subsidy provided to students rather than to address an actual increase in costs.

Congress has proposed addressing college prices via college costs through incentive programs. For example, a demonstration program could provide grants to consortia of institutions working together to reduce costs (e.g., by sharing administrative functions or purchasing health care collectively).[98] As previously discussed, institutions are already forming these consortia on their own, but it is possible that more consortia would be formed if incentives to do so existed. It might also be useful to examine the levels of costs savings and areas in which cost savings have been achieved by existing consortia to help determine how to structure an effective incentive.

Encouraging institutions to control costs might be more appealing and more feasible than other routes for controlling price increases, but these strategies may not have as large an impact on prices as desired, as productivity gains in labor-intensive enterprises are difficult to obtain. In addition, efforts to control costs could inadvertently result in diminished quality and quantity of courses, programs, and services. Finally, providing funding directly to institutions as incentives to increase college affordability rather than to students through the federal student aid system has not been the primary traditional role of the federal government in higher education. In general, however, Congress has not focused as intensively on college costs as it has on college prices, but it could be argued that college costs could be addressed indirectly by legislation focused on college prices. That is, by encouraging institutions to reduce their price increases, institutions may find it necessary to also reduce their cost increases.

EARNING COLLEGE CREDITS

Another approach to making college more affordable for students focuses on the development of articulation agreements, the transfer of credits, dual enrollment, and programs to help students finish their coursework. Although many of these proposals also represent actions that could be taken by states and institutions, Congress may continue to examine ways to encourage these practices.

These types of measures may result in cost savings to institutions and reduce the overall price students pay for higher education. For example, articulation agreements (also known as cooperative agreements), transfer agreements, and transfer of credit agreements, are generally established to facilitate students' transfer of credit from one postsecondary institution to another. They are intended to help students understand which of their credits may be accepted at another institution; reduce the time, effort, and money required to review transcripts and determine compatibility between courses; reduce the number of courses that a student may need to repeat, thereby saving the student time and money; and potentially reduce the amount of federal aid needed by a student to complete an education.[99]

Congress could also consider addressing the transfer of credit issue more specifically by requiring institutions to make public their transfer of credit policies or place restrictions on these policies, such as prohibiting institutions from denying the transfer of credit on the basis of the accreditation held by the sending institution.[100] While transfer of credit requirements may be helpful to students in many of the same ways that articulation agreements are beneficial, they may also result in increased costs at IHEs that had previously made decisions about the transfer of credit on the basis of the accreditation held by the sending institution. That is, if IHEs were required to examine every transfer applicant's transcripts on an individual basis, it could increase the amount of time and effort needed to make a determination about the transfer of credit. These costs could potentially be passed on to students, resulting in increased tuition and fees. The use of articulation agreements, however, could help to reduce these potential burdens, and widely publishing institutions' transfer of credit policies may help students make more informed decisions about their postsecondary education.

Relieving Regulatory Burden

Regulations encompass requirements that function as control strategies (e.g., accountability measures), but these regulations often add to the costs institutions shoulder in providing higher education to students. Postsecondary institutions and some researchers have agreed that institutions may already be overburdened by regulation. Most agree that public accountability is essential, but there are questions about whether public accountability could be maintained through less costly and cumbersome measures and whether the related savings would be passed on to students. For example, performance-based models and requirements could be implemented, allowing institutions to determine how to meet specific requirements, rather than specifying both standards and procedures for meeting standards. Congress has previously considered implementing a demonstration program that would have supported innovative approaches in the delivery of higher education and student financial aid at reduced costs for students and institutions.[101] A specific goal of the program would have been to identify specific statutory and regulatory requirements that should be modified to allow for the more efficient and effective delivery of federal student aid, as well as to provide access to distance education, to enable students to complete their postsecondary education more efficiently. It is possible that continued consideration may be given to relieving regulatory burden as Congress continues work on HEA reauthorization.[102]

Providing Better Public Information

Another possible approach to the issues of price and cost is to provide potential and current students with more and better information about these issues, enabling them to make more informed decisions about their postsecondary education; that is, providing information to enable the higher education market to operate more efficiently without controls or incentives. Some information is available to the general public through various college guides and websites, but concerns have been raised by researchers that there is not enough information available. It has also been suggested that data related to college costs and price should be designed to be useful, accurate, timely, and understandable. On the basis of the bills already introduced by Congress related to these issues,[103] Congress may continue to consider how to make better information more readily available to current and prospective students.

While Congress may consider addressing the need for more useful information to be made available to the public (e.g., additional data on instructional expenditures, completion and graduation rates, or faculty information), it might do so by building on existing data collection strategies. Current legislation mandates that the National Center for Education Statistics (NCES) collect data from postsecondary institutions and that institutions respond to the Integrated Postsecondary Education Data System (IPEDS) surveys in a timely manner. There are some concerns, however, that institutions do not respond appropriately to IPEDS.[104] In addition, there are time lags between when the data are collected and released to the public. This could be a problem, however, with any data collection designed to include the universe of institutions.

In addition, existing HEA legislation requires institutions to provide current and prospective students and their families with a variety of institutional information.[105] While institutions are required to tell enrolled students what information is available, Congress could consider strengthening existing requirements by specifying how data must be presented in terms of user-friendly formats and how individuals must be notified about the existence of the data and how to easily obtain it. There also is discussion of adding additional accountability measures for institutions. If these measures are added, provisions could be made to ensure that this information is made available to students and their families.

The U.S. Department of Education currently maintains an online database of information about postsecondary institutions known as the College Navigator.[106] Congress could use the College Navigator as one venue for making any additional information about postsecondary institutions available to the public and could consider whether changes are needed in the design of the website or in the information presented on the current site to improve the usefulness of the data.

APPENDIX. AVERAGE UNDERGRADUATE TUITION AND FEES

Table A-1. Average Undergraduate Tuition and Required Fees, Charged for Full-Time Students in Degree-Granting Institutions, by Type and Control of Institution 1976-1977 to 2005-2006 (in constant 2005 dollars)

Year	All Institutions			Public Institutions			Private Institutions		
	All	Four-Year	Two-Year	All	Four-Year	Two-Year	All	Four-Year	Two-Year
1976-1977	$3,172	$4,182	$1,186	$1,643	$2,117	$973	$8,467	$8,698	$5,464
1977-1978	3,173	4,162	1,219	1,649	2,110	988	8,456	8,702	5,496
1978-1979	3,213	4,184	1,231	1,626	2,060	980	8,589	8,860	5,484
1979-1980	3,128	4,070	1,213	1,569	1,984	954	8,420	8,676	5,546
1980-1981	3,054	3,979	1,246	1,505	1,905	927	8,291	8,572	5,719
1981-1982	3,130	4,098	1,267	1,534	1,954	934	8,49	8,838	5,596
1982-1983	3,290	4,330	1,365	1,615	2,087	957	8,983	9,388	6,088
1983-1984	3,496	4,595	1,432	1,748	2,251	1,035	9,511	9,986	6,077
1984-1985	3,732	4,826	1,544	1,825	2,308	1,098	9,990	10,443	6,551
1985-1986	3,959	5,054	1,613	1,896	2,392	1,163	10,507	11,109	6,665
1986-1987	4,120	5,421	1,599	1,971	2,519	1,177	11,254	11,865	6,564
1987-1988	4,226	5,503	1,391	2,094	2,643	1,213	12,014	12,234	7,153
1988-1989	4,387	5,732	1,617	2,121	2,718	1,205	12,317	12,747	7,953
1989-1990	4,472	5,985	1,540	2,136	2,803	1,191	12,832	13,224	8,184
1990-1991	4,507	5,990	1,625	2,173	2,821	1,231	13,108	13,572	8,323
1991-1992	4,711	6,288	1,705	2,334	3,035	1,343	13,507	13,994	8,251
1992-1993	4,896	6,615	1,776	2,480	3,270	1,427	13,839	14,329	8,434
1993-1994	5,173	6,919	1,890	2,625	3,428	1,520	14,288	14,803	8,609

Table A-1. (Continued)

Year	All Institutions			Public Institutions			Private Institutions		
	All	Four-Year	Two-Year	All	Four-Year	Two-Year	All	Four-Year	Two-Year
1994-1995	5,330	7,104	1,960	2,711	3,533	1,571	14,642	15,130	9,112
1995-1996	5,559	7,415	1,951	2,792	3,649	1,588	15,204	15,690	9,092
1996-1997	5,681	7,616	1,921	2,827	3,718	1,588	15,557	16,034	9,007
1997-1998	5,786	7,727	2,062	2,872	3,784	1,599	15,576	16,238	9,083
1998-1999	6,006	8,055	2,067	2,912	3,869	1,589	16,089	16,742	9,410
1999-2000	6,140	8,257	2,018	2,937	3,926	1,568	16,506	17,102	9,653
2000-2001	6,099	8,360	1,926	2,906	3,970	1,511	17,013	17,546	10,283
2001-2002	6,227	8,586	1,985	2,978	4,119	1,522	17,360	17,877	11,112
2002-2003	6,516	9,020	2,066	3,151	4,393	1,610	17,785	18,266	11,563
2003-2004	7,013	9,582	2,308	3,523	4,868	1,806	18,391	18,869	12,255
2004-2005	7,363	10,035	2,417	3,752	5,197	1,911	18,769	19,234	12,533
2005-2006	7,601	10,279	2,417	3,874	5,351	1,935	18,862	19,292	12,450

Source: CRS analysis based on U.S. Department of Education, National Center for Education Statistics, *Digest of Education Statistics 2002*, Table 319, at [http://www.nces.ed.gov/]; and Bureau of Labor Statistics, annual unadjusted Consumer Price Index-Urban data, at [http://www.bls.gov/].

Note: All data are reported in constant 2005 dollars.

REFERENCES

[1] John Immerwahr and Jean Johnson, *Squeeze Play: How Parents and the Public Look at Higher Education Today*, by Public Agenda for the National Center for Public Policy and Higher Education, May 31, 2007.

[2] Of the approximately 18 million individuals enrolled in higher education in the fall of 2005, nearly 55% were full-time undergraduates, 31% were part-time undergraduates, and the remaining 14% were full- or part-time graduate students. (U.S. Department of Education, National Center for Education Statistics, "Enrollment in Postsecondary Institutions, Fall 2005; Graduation Rates, 1999 and 2002 Cohorts; and Financial Statistics, Fiscal Year 2005," NCES 2007-154, April 2007, pp. 4-5, Table 1.)

[3] U.S. Department of Education, National Center for Education Statistics, *Digest of Education Statistics 2006.* NCES-2007-017, July 2007. Table 319. (Hereafter cited as ED, *Digest 2006*).

[4] CRS analysis based on U.S. Department of Education, National Center for Education Statistics, *Digest of Education Statistics 2006*, Table 319, at [http://www.nces.ed.gov/]; Bureau of Labor Statistics, annual unadjusted Consumer Price Index-Urban (CPI-U) data, available at [http://www.bls.gov/]; and U.S. Census Bureau, Historical Income Tables —Households, Table H-6, at [http://www.census.gov/hhes/www/income/histinc/h06ar.html], and Table H-3, at [http://www.census.gov/hhes/www/income/histinc/h03ar.html].

[5] COA is used in determining federal student aid packages. For more information on COA, see CRS Report RL33266, *Federal Student Aid Need Analysis System: Background, Description, and Legislative Action*, by Charmaine Mercer.

[6] An effort will be made to distinguish whether a reference is being made to price net of grant aid only or to price net all student aid.

[7] The use of expenditures in this report as a measure of college costs should not be interpreted to imply that these expenditures are

necessarily efficient. No analysis or judgment about what it costs to provide a service is made.

[8] ED, *Digest 2006*, Table 339.

[9] ED, *Digest 2006*, Tables 336 and 337.

[10] Ibid.

[11] D.W. Breneman, "An Essay on College Costs" in U.S. Department of Education, National Center for Education Statistics, 2001, *Study of College Costs and Prices, 1988-89 to 1997-98, Volume 2: Commissioned Papers*, available at [http://nces.ed.gov/pubsearch/ pubsinfo. asp?pubid=2002157]. (Hereafter referred to as ED, *Costs and Prices Volume 2*.)

[12] ED, *Digest 2006,* Table 176.

[13] By comparison, expenditures on instruction in 1980-1981 at public degree-granting institutions accounted for 35% of expenditures. Historical data showing expenditures for instruction are reported only for all private degree-granting institutions as opposed to being reported separately for private not-for-profit and private for-profit institutions for 1980-1981. The percentage of expenditures on instruction for all private degree-granting institutions in 1980-1981 was 27% (ED, *Digest 2006*, Table 345).

[14] ED, *Digest 2006*, Table 354.

[15] Scholarships and fellowships only include funds provided in the form of outright grants and training stipends to students enrolled in formal coursework. This is referred to as net grant aid in Table 2.

[16] ED, *Digest 2006*, Table 347.

[17] The College Board, *Trends in College Pricing*, 2007, figure 1, at [http://www.college board.com/prod_downloads/about/news_info/trends/trends_pricing_07 .pdf].

[18] American Council on Education, *Attitudes Toward Public Higher Education National Survey Results*, 2002, at [http://www.acenet. edu/news/press_release/2002/02february/ national.data.ppt].

[19] For more information on subsidies, see, for example, G.C. Winston, "Higher Education's Costs, Prices, and Subsidies: Some Economic Facts and Fundamentals" in U.S. Department of Education, National Center for Education Statistics, 2001, *Study of College Costs and Prices, 1988-89 to 1997-98 Volume 2: Commissioned Papers*, at [http://www.nces.ed.gov/ pubsearch/pubsinfo.asp?pubid=2002157]. (Hereafter cited as ED, *Costs and Prices Volume 2*.)

[20] This analysis assumes that students do not receive grant, loan, or other types of student financial assistance beyond the subsidy.

[21] This assumes that the entire $8,000 received in state appropriations for each student is used to offset the cost of providing education. There is some debate in the literature about whether this actually occurs. For

example, some researchers argue that revenue may be diverted for other purposes, such as faculty or graduate student use. See D.W. Breneman, "An Essay on College Costs" in ED, *Costs and Prices Volume 2*.

[22] For more details about current out-of-state tuition setting policies, see State Higher Education Executive Officers, 2006, *State Tuition, Fees, and Financial Assistance Policies, 2005-2006*, at [http://www.sheeo.org]. (Hereafter cited as SHEEO, *State Tuition and Fees*.)

[23] Changes in tuition in constant dollars are addressed in a subsequent section.

[24] In this example, four-year public universities are used because continuous data are available for this type of institution. *Universities* are the subset of four-year public institutions that are often the most prominent in the state, consisting of an undergraduate college, diverse graduate programs, and professional schools. Regardless of recent mission expansions at some other four-year institutions, NCES has not expanded the list of universities since 1982.

[25] CRS calculations from data in ED, *Digest 2006*, Table 319.

[26] Note, however, that as tuition and fees increase over time, subsequent increases in tuition and fees of the same dollar amount result in lower percentage increases. For example, if tuition and fees increased from $1,000 to $2,000 over 10 years, an increase of $1,000 or 100%, a subsequent $1,000 increase over the next 10 years from $2,000 to $3,000 will result in only a 50% increase in tuition and fees.

[27] The CPI-U is a measure of the average change in prices paid by urban consumers for specific goods and services. It is often used as a proxy measure for the cost of living. See CRS Report RL30074, *The Consumer Price Index: A Brief Overview*, by Brian W. Cashell.

[28] See, for example, the National Center for Public Policy and Higher Education, *Losing Ground: A National Status Report on the Affordability of American Higher Education*, 2002.

[29] Net price is discussed in the next section of this report.

[30] The College Board, *Trends in Student Aid 2007*, October 2007, at [http://www.college board.com/prod_downloads/about/news_info/trends/trends_aid_07.pdf]. (Hereafter cited as The College Board, *Student Aid*.)

[31] Ibid.

[32] For more information on tax deductions and credits, see CRS Report RL31129, *Higher Education Tax Credits and Deduction: An Overview of the Benefits and Their Relationship to Traditional Student Aid*, by Linda Levine and Adam Stoll. For more information on tax benefits for college savings, see CRS Report RL32155, *Tax-Favored Higher Education Savings Benefits and Their Relationship to Traditional Federal Student Aid*, by Linda Levine and Charmaine Mercer. Also

see CRS Report RS21870, *Education Tax Benefits: Are They Permanent or Temporary?*, by Linda Levine.

[33] Federal student aid authorized by Title IV of the HEA is only available to students attending eligible institutions of higher education. For more information about institutional eligibility for Title IV programs, see CRS Report RL31926, *Institutional Eligibility for Participation in Title IV Student Aid Programs Under the Higher Education Act: Background and Issues*, by Rebecca Skinner.

[34] For an overview of the smaller federal aid programs authorized in the HEA, see CRS Report RL34214, *A Primer on the Higher Education Act (HEA)*, by Charmaine Mercer and Rebecca R. Skinner.

[35] For more information, see CRS Report RL31668, *Federal Pell Grant Program of the Higher Education Act: Background and Reauthorization*, by Charmaine Mercer.

[36] For more information, see CRS Report RL33673, *Federal Family Education Loan Program and William D. Ford Direct Loan Program Student Loans: Terms and Conditions for Borrowers*, by Adam Stoll.

[37] ED, *Digest 2006*, Table 327.

[38] The College Board, *Student Aid*.

[39] U.S. Department of Education, National Center for Education Statistics, *Student Financing of Undergraduate Education: 2003-04: With a Special Analysis of the Net Price of Attendance and Federal Education Tax Benefits*, NCES 2006-186, 2006, at [http://www.nces.ed.gov/pubs2006/2006186.pdf].

[40] Data for private for-profit institutions were not disaggregated by level.

[41] ED, *Costs and Prices Volume 1*, p. 21.

[42] See for example, Testimony of Sandy Baum, U.S. House of Representatives, Committee on Education and the Workforce, Subcommittee on 21st Century Competitiveness, *Affordability in Higher Education: We Know There's a Problem; What's the Solution?*, hearing, July 10, 2003, at [http://edworkforce.house.gov/ hearings/108th/21st/afford71003/ baum.htm]. (Hereafter cited as House Education and the Workforce, *Affordability in Higher Education*.)

[43] ED, *Costs and Prices Volume 1*, p. 21.

[44] See House Education and the Workforce, *Affordability in Higher Education*; or The National Commission on the Cost of Higher Education, *Straight Talk About College Costs and Prices*, 1998, at [http://www.eriche.org/government/talk.html]. (Hereafter cited as NCC, *College Costs and Prices*.)

[45] According to a recent SHEEO survey of state higher education agencies, most of the responding agencies (41 of 46) reported charging different levels of tuition for undergraduate and graduate students, and 32 of 46 agencies reported charging different prices for credit and non-

credit bearing enrollment. For more information, see SHEEO, *State Tuition and Fees*.

[46] SHEEO, *State Tuition and Fees*.

[47] Ibid. Note that states may have identified more than one tuition-setting authority, reflecting differences in policy among various state institutions.

[48] See for example, SHEEO, *State Tuition and Fees*; IHEP, *Reauthorizing HEA*; and ED, *Costs and Prices Volume 1*.

[49] SHEEO, *State Tuition and Fees*.

[50] For example, limits on tuition increases may be instituted or encouraged by state legislatures, governors, or institutions.

[51] IHEP, *Reauthorizing HEA*, p. 117.

[52] All data on state tax funds appropriated for higher education operating expenses were provided by the Center for the Study of Education Policy, Illinois State University, available at [http://www.grapevine.ilstu.edu/fifty_state_summary.htm]. Appropriations for capital outlays and debt service are not included in the total amounts reported by states. In addition, appropriation of funds derived from federal sources, student fees, auxiliary enterprises, and other non-tax sources were also excluded.

[53] Ibid.

[54] IHEP, *Reauthorizing HEA*, p. 116-117.

[55] In the 1980s, the U.S. Department of Justice launched an investigation into possible antitrust violations by private institutions. The primary focus of the investigation was on the 23 institutions, including all of the Ivy League universities, composing the Overlap Group, which met annually to compare financial aid offers made to students admitted to two or more member institutions. As a result of the suit, the institutions discontinued their collaboration with respect to financial aid packages. Through the Higher Education Act, however, Congress has authorized an exemption for institutions that do not consider a family's ability to pay in making admissions decisions (need-blind admissions) to permit them to discuss their financial aid policies. The exemption currently is approved until 2008 (P.L. 107-72).

[56] The NCES study only included private not-for-profit four-year institutions. Private not-for-profit two-year institutions and private for-profit institutions were not examined. (U.S. Department of Education, National Center for Education Statistics, 2001, *Study of College Costs and Prices, 1988-89 to 1997-98 Volume 1*, available at [http://www.nces.ed.gov/pubsearch/pubsinfo.asp?pubid=2002157]. (Hereafter cited as ED, *Costs and Prices Volume 1*.)

[57] For more information on tuition discounting, see L. Lapovsky, *Institutional Financial Health: Tuition Discounting and Enrollment Management*, in ED, *Costs and Prices Volume 2*.

[58] Lumina Foundation for Education, *Unintended Consequences of Tuition Discounting*, May 2003, at [http://www.luminafoundation.org/publications/Tuitiondiscounting.pdf].
[59] ED, *Costs and Prices Volume 1.*
[60] For more information about federal grants and loans, see, for example, CRS Report RL30655, *Federal Student Loans: Terms and Conditions for Borrowers*, by Adam Stoll; and CRS Report RL31668, *Federal Pell Grant Program of the Higher Education Act: Background and Reauthorization*, by Charmaine Mercer.
[61] Incentives for price increases also may be created when grant and loan limits are increased and an institution currently charges a price below these levels.
[62] ED, *Costs and Prices Volume I.*
[63] For the purposes of this study, the researchers developed a modified version of the Carnegie classification codes. Comprehensive institutions include institutions offering a full range of bachelor's programs that are also committed to graduate education through the master's degree. These institutions award 20 or more master's degrees annually in one or more disciplines.
[64] The aforementioned NCES study of college costs and prices did not include federal tax credits in its analysis.
[65] Government Accountability Office (then called General Accounting Office), September 2002, *Student Aid and Tax Benefits: Better Research and Guidance Will Facilitate Comparison and Effectiveness of Student Use*, GAO-02-751, at [http://www.gao.gov/].
[66] SHEEO, *State Tuition and Fees*.
[67] B.T. Long, "The Impact of Federal Tax Credits for Higher Education Expenses" in Caroline M. Hoxby, ed., *College Costs: The Economics of Which College, When, College, and How to Pay for It*, Chicago: University of Chicago Press, 2004. (Hereafter cited as Long, *Impact of Federal Tax Credits*.)
[68] Ibid.
[69] For examples of recommendations of state and institutional strategies that could be implemented to address the issues of college costs and price, see Commission on the Future of Higher Education, 2006, *A Test of Leadership: Charting the Future of U.S. Higher Education*, at [http://www.ed.gov/about/bdscomm/list/hiedfuture/index.html];
Dickerson, R.C., 2004, *Collision Course: Rising College Costs Threaten America's Future and Require Shared Solutions,* at [http://www.collegecosts.info/]; and Lumina Foundation, 2005, *Course Corrections: Experts Offer Solutions to the College Cost Crisis*, Indianapolis, IN: Author.
[70] Fischer, K. "Well-Heeled U. Of Virginia Tries to Balance Access With Prestige." *Chronicle of Higher Education*, May 12, 2006.

[71] Fischer, K. "Colorado's 'Noble Experiment.'" *Chronicle of Higher Education*, July 15, 2005.
[72] Ibid.
[73] For more information, see University of Illinois Guaranteed Tuition Plan Summary, at [http://www.vpaa.uillinois.edu/policies/tuition_guarantee_summary.pdf].
[74] Hebel, S. "Push for Tuition Predictability." *Chronicle of Higher Education*, May 20, 2005.
[75] As previously discussed, as institutions implement strategies to reduce costs, the general concern is a reduction in the quality of the education and services provided to students.
[76] Gose, G. "Colleges Rely on Consortia, Contractors, and Ingenuity to Cut Costs." *The Chronicle of Higher Education*, January 27, 2006. (Hereafter referred to as *Chronicle*, "Consortia, Contractors, and Ingenuity.")
[77] *Chronicle*, "Consortia, Contractors, and Ingenuity."
[78] Ekman, R. "Many Small Private Colleges Thrive with Modest Endowments." *The Chronicle of Higher Education*, June 2, 2006.
[79] *Chronicle*, "Consortia, Contractors, and Ingenuity."
[80] Ibid.
[81] IHEP, *Reauthorizing the HEA*.
[82] Ibid.
[83] *Chronicle*, "Consortia, Contractors, and Ingenuity."
[84] Hale, G. (2001). *Postsecondary Options: Dual/Concurrent Enrollment*. Available online from the Education Commission of the states at [http://www.ecs.org/clearinghouse/28/ 11/2811.doc].
[85] Mellon, E. "Extra Effort in the Classroom Pays Off: International Baccalaureate Puts Participants on College Fast Track." *Houston Chronicle*: January 4, 2007.
[86] Based on an analysis of the use of articulation agreements in all 50 states conducted by CRS in December 2006.
[87] Based on findings from an unpublished analysis conducted by CRS.
[88] Based on findings from an unpublished analysis conducted by CRS.
[89] Education Commission of the States, *Articulation and Transfer*, [http://www.community collegepolicy.org/html/toolkit/articulation/].
[90] NCC, *College Costs and Prices*, p. 21. The National Commission on the Cost of Higher Education argues against a one-size-fits-all approach for reducing price or controlling costs.
[91] See for example, S. 1642 in the 110th Congress and H.R. 609 and S. 1614 in the 109th Congress.
[92] For more information, see [http://www.bls.gov/cpi/home. htm#overview].
[93] These indices may be calculated at [http://data.bls.gov/PDQ/outside. jsp?survey=cu].

[94] The discussion of the HEPI is based on information available from the Commonfund, *College and University Higher Education Price Index, 2004 Update*, at [http://www.commonfund.org/ Templates/ InvestorServices/RESOURCE_REQUEST/ target.pdf?RES_GUID=2CE78A52-3B56-40E6-8744-CCE745989978]. (Hereafter referred to as Commonfund, *HEPI*.)

[95] The Commonfund Institute focuses on providing nonprofit organizations with investment information and professional development programs. It is the education and research arm of the Commonfund, an investment firm.

[96] Commonfund, *HEPI*, p. 16.

[97] HEPI was originally based on 25 budget components that were organized in 8 categories (e.g., professional salaries, non-professional wages, contracted services, utilities).

[98] For example, see S. 371 in the 109th Congress.

[99] For example, H.R. 2739 and H.R. 2960 in the 109th Congress would have established articulation agreement demonstration programs. S. 1642 in the 110th Congress would require institutions to provide to current and prospective students a list of other institutions with which they have established articulation agreements.

[100] For examples of proposed transfer of credit policies, see S. 1642 in the 110th Congress and H.R. 609 and S. 1614 in the 109th Congress. For more information about transfer of credit issues, see CRS Report RL32989, *Accreditation and Reauthorization of the Higher Education Act*, by Rebecca R. Skinner and Jody Feder.

[101] See for example, H.R. 609 in the 109th Congress.

[102] See for example, H.R. 3746 in the 110th Congress.

[103] See for example, S. 1642 and H.R. 3746 in the 110th Congress and H.R. 609 and S. 1614 in the 109th Congress.

[104] In July 2003, ED announced that about 470 institutions had failed to complete at least one of the 10 IPEDS surveys. In August 2003, ED announced that it was fining about 80 institutions.

[105] HEA, Section 485.

[106] The College Navigator was formerly known as the College Opportunities On-Line (COOL) website.

INDEX

D

E

F

Q

R

S

T

U

V

W